TEAM SPIRIT®

SMART BOOKS FOR YOUNG FANS

THE WASHINGTON REDSKINS

BY
MARK STEWART

New Hanover County Public Library
201 Chestnut Street
Wilmington, North Carolina 28401

NORWOOD HOUSE PRESS
CHICAGO, ILLINOIS

Norwood House Press
P.O. Box 316598
Chicago, Illinois 60631

For information regarding Norwood House Press, please visit our website at:
www.norwoodhousepress.com or call 866-565-2900.

All photos courtesy of Getty Images except the following:
Icon SMI (4), Washington Redskins (7),
Black Book Partners (10, 11, 14, 22, 23, 25, 30, 31, 35 top left & bottom, 39, 43 top),
Topps, Inc. (15, 34 right, 38, 42 top left, 45), National Chicle (17, 20), Philadelphia Gum Co. (21),
Author's Collection (33, 36, 37, 43 bottom), Bowman Gum Co. (34 left), SCH Publications (41),
Lexington Library, Inc. (42 bottom left), Matt Richman (48).
Cover Photo: Icon SMI

The memorabilia and artifacts pictured in this book are presented for educational and informational purposes,
and come from the collection of the author.

Editor: Mike Kennedy
Designer: Ron Jaffe
Project Management: Black Book Partners, LLC.
Special thanks to Topps, Inc.

Library of Congress Cataloging-in-Publication Data

Stewart, Mark, 1960-
  The Washington Redskins / by Mark Stewart. -- Rev. ed.
    p. cm. -- (Team spirit)
  Includes bibliographical references and index.
  Summary: "A revised Team Spirit Football edition featuring the Washington
Redskins that chronicles the history and accomplishments of the team.
Includes access to the Team Spirit website which provides additional
information and photos"--Provided by publisher.
  ISBN 978-1-59953-543-2 (library edition : alk. paper) -- ISBN
978-1-60357-485-3 (ebook)
 1. Washington Redskins (Football team)--History--Juvenile literature. I.
Title.
  GV956.W3S74 2012
  796.332'6409753--dc23
                                                    2012016872

Manufactured in the United States of America in North Mankato, Minnesota.
205N—082012

COVER PHOTO: The Redskins line up on offense to run a play.

Table of Contents

ABOUT OUR GLOSSARY

In this book, there may be several words that you are reading for the first time. Some are sports words, some are new vocabulary words, and some are familiar words that are used in an unusual way. All of these words are defined on page 46. Throughout the book, sports words appear in **bold type**. Regular vocabulary words appear in *bold italic type*.

Meet the Redskins

Some teams in the **National Football League (NFL)** constantly try new ideas in the hope of winning. The Washington Redskins prefer to stick with the proven way. They make powerful blocks, jarring tackles, and battle over every yard. Near the end of most games, their opponents are huffing and puffing while the Redskins are getting their *second wind*.

More than 70 years ago, when the Redskins played their first game in Washington, D.C., *professional* football was just trying to survive. Today it is the country's favorite sport. The Redskins are an important part of that success story. They were popular from the first time they took the field. Now they are a bigger hit than ever.

This book tells the story of the Redskins. They are not a team for fans of clean uniforms. The dirtier the Redskins are, the happier they feel and the better they play. Call it *tradition*. Call it *superstition*. Better yet, just call it Redskins football.

The Redskins celebrate a touchdown. They have a history as an offensive powerhouse.

Glory Days

The NFL was not yet 10 years old when the **_Great Depression_** hit the United States. Most fans could no longer afford to attend games, and the league struggled to stay in business. Fortunately for the NFL, a man named George Preston Marshall believed that pro football would be a success in the long run. Marshall was a wealthy businessman from the Washington, D.C. area. In 1932, he

bought a team in Boston, Massachusetts, and named it the Braves. A year later he changed the name to the Redskins.

The Redskins were a good team. Their early stars included Turk Edwards, Cliff Battles, Ernie Pinckert, Jim Musick, and Wayne Millner. Still, Marshall could not find a way to fill the stands in Boston. In 1937, he moved the Redskins "home" to Washington. That season, they signed their first great passer, Sammy Baugh.

With Baugh leading the way, Washington finished atop the NFL's **East Division** in 1937 and four more times from 1940 to 1945. The Redskins were league champions in 1937 and 1942. The stars of those great teams included ends Bob Masterson and Joe Aguirre, plus linemen Dick Farman, Steve Slivinski, and Willie Wilkin.

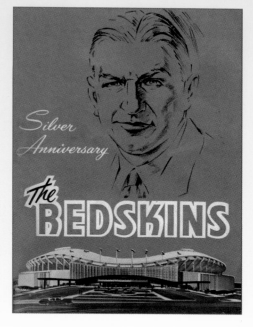

After Baugh retired, the Redskins fell on hard times. In the years after **World War II**, they enjoyed only two winning seasons despite having plenty of stars. In the 1950s and early 1960s, Washington had talent up and down its roster, including quarterbacks Eddie LeBaron and Norm Snead, running backs Charlie Justice and Don Bosseler, and receivers Hugh Taylor and Bill Anderson. The team's defensive leaders were Gene Brito and Chuck Drazenovich.

Perhaps the biggest reason for Washington's poor record was Marshall's unwillingness to sign African-American players. During the nation's racial tension of the 1960s, he feared that white fans would not root for black players. It took a personal plea from President

LEFT: Sammy Baugh prepares to throw a long pass.
ABOVE: George Preston Marshall is pictured on the team's 1962 yearbook.

John F. Kennedy to convince Marshall that he was wrong. The Redskins soon added talented African-American stars such as Bobby Mitchell, Charley Taylor, and Larry Brown.

By the 1970s, the Redskins were transformed into a championship contender. They relied on a mix of young stars and veterans, including quarterbacks Billy Kilmer and Sonny Jurgensen, safety Pat Fischer, and linebacker Chris Hanburger. The team rose to the top of the **National Football Conference (NFC)** in 1972 and played in **Super Bowl** VII.

The Redskins were even better in the 1980s and 1990s, after they hired Joe Gibbs to coach the team. Gibbs was a football genius who worked as hard as anyone in the NFL. He always got the best out of his players. Those teams were led by four talented quarterbacks—Joe Theismann, Jay Schroeder, Doug Williams, and Mark Rypien. Their other stars included John Riggins, Art Monk, Darrell Green, Charles Mann, and Mark Moseley.

Washington's best weapon was its offensive line. Nicknamed the "Hogs," they were the best blockers in the NFL for many years.

LEFT: Joe Gibbs poses with the three Super Bowl trophies that he won as Washington's coach.   **ABOVE**: The Hogs surround Joe Theismann and John Riggins.

The Redskins were not always an exciting team to watch, but their fans loved them because they were winners. Washington played in four Super Bowls during this period and won three of them.

Gibbs retired after the 1992 season. The Redskins hired some talented coaches in the **decade** that followed, including Norv Turner, Marty Schottenheimer, and Steve Spurrier. Some excellent players wore the burgundy and gold, such as LaVar Arrington, Stephen Davis, Chris Samuels, and Ken Harvey. However, Washington won just one **NFC East** title after 1992.

In 2004, team owner Daniel Snyder convinced Gibbs to return to coaching. The two hoped to recapture the team's glory days. They had the talent to do so. Clinton Portis and Santana Moss gave the team two great weapons on offense, and Marcus Washington

led an improving defense. Gibbs guided the Redskins back to the **playoffs** twice in three seasons, but he later decided to hang up his clipboard for good.

Since then, the Redskins have tried to find the right mix of **veteran** leaders and young stars. Players such as Brian Orakpo, Ryan Kerrigan, Trent Williams, and Fred Davis learned the "Washington way" from the time they were **rookies**. They passed on their wisdom to up-and-coming players, including Robert Griffin III. The Redskins took him with the second pick of the 2012 **draft**. He gave the fans hope for a bright future.

LEFT: Clinton Portis   **ABOVE**: Brian Orakpo

Home Turf

When they were in Boston, the Redskins played in Fenway Park, which was also home to baseball's Red Sox. After their move to Washington, the Redskins used Griffith Stadium and then D.C. Stadium, which was later renamed Robert F. Kennedy Stadium. They played there for more than 30 years.

In 1997, the team moved to a new stadium in Landover, Maryland. The game is only part of the experience there. Thousands of fans enter the stadium two hours before kickoff to enjoy the live music provided by the team. After every game—win or lose—the Redskins throw a two-hour "fifth quarter" party under the stands.

BY THE NUMBERS

- The Redskins' stadium has 91,000 seats.
- The stadium cost $250.5 million to build.
- The stadium has five levels of seats. Each level is named after an important person in team history.

The seat colors in the Redskins' stadium match the colors of the team's uniforms.

Dressed for Success

The Redskins love tradition. For more than 70 years, their uniforms have featured a combination of **burgundy** and gold. In their early years, the players wore gold pants and a dark jersey with the likeness of a Native American on the front. Today, the Redskins are one of the few teams that prefer to wear their white uniforms at home and dark uniforms on the road. Joe Gibbs started this tradition in 1981.

Originally, the Redskins wore burgundy helmets with no **logo** on the sides. The team added a feather design in the 1950s and later changed to a spear design. Washington switched to an *R* inside a circle in 1970. The Redskins began using their current logo two years later.

Some believe the word "Redskin" is an insult to the native peoples of North America. The Redskins believe their name **symbolizes** a proud tradition and do not plan to change it.

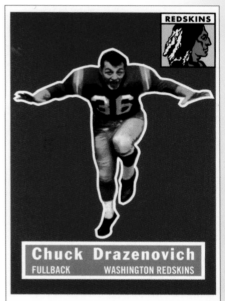

Chuck Drazenovich
FULLBACK   WASHINGTON REDSKINS

LEFT: DeAngelo Hall wears the team's white home jersey.
RIGHT: This trading card of Chuck Drazenovich shows the team's home uniform from the 1950s.

15

The Redskins never won a championship while they played in Boston. But they made a great impression with the fans in Washington. In 1937, their first season there, the Redskins captured the NFL championship.

A rookie quarterback named Sammy Baugh led the team. He was called "Slingin' Sammy" because of the way he passed the ball all over the field to his receivers. Baugh also played running back, so he was in total command of the Washington offense. He would take a handoff and either run, pass, or punt. On defense, Baugh was one of the best pass defenders in the NFL.

The Redskins also had Cliff Battles in their **backfield**. He was the league's top runner that year. Battles and Baugh led Washington against the Chicago Bears for the 1937 title. The game was exciting from the opening kickoff. The Bears were ahead at halftime, but the

LEFT: Cliff Battles and Wayne Millner congratulate Sammy Baugh after their 1937 championship.
RIGHT: Turk Edwards was an important team leader during the 1930s.

Redskins fought back. Baugh threw three touchdown passes in the third quarter, and the Washington defense shut out the Bears the rest of the game. The Redskins celebrated their first championship with a 28–21 victory. Baugh passed for 354 yards, which broke the record for the NFL title game.

Washington's next championship came in 1942. The Redskins faced the Bears again. This time, they won by a score of 14–6. The game turned in the second quarter when Baugh threw a 39-yard touchdown pass to Wilbur Moore. Andy Farkas capped off a scoring drive in the third quarter to give the Redskins the lead for good.

Washington fans had to wait 40 years before they could celebrate another championship. In 1982, Russ Grimm, Joe Jacoby, and Jeff Bostic formed the heart of an offensive line known as the Hogs. They created huge openings for running back John Riggins and gave quarterback Joe Theismann all the time he needed to pass.

In January of 1983, the Redskins met the Miami Dolphins in Super Bowl XVII. Washington trailed 17–13 in the fourth quarter and faced a fourth down on Miami's 43-yard line. Coach Joe Gibbs decided to try for a first down. Riggins took a handoff, cut around the left side of the line, ran over a tackler, and sprinted into the end zone for the winning touchdown. The Redskins went on to win, 27–17.

Five years later, Washington made another impressive run for the NFL championship. The Redskins had a balanced offense and a tough defense. Quarterback Doug Williams took over for Jay Schroeder late in the season. Williams proved to be a perfect fit.

The Redskins faced the Denver Broncos in Super Bowl XXII. The fans expected a great day from Denver quarterback John Elway. Instead, they saw Williams make history. He tossed four touchdown passes in the second quarter on the way to a 42–10 victory. Running back Timmy Smith, another Washington substitute, ran for 204 yards and two touchdowns.

The Redskins won their fifth championship four seasons later. They raced through the regular season with a 14–2 record. Quarterback Mark Rypien threw 28 touchdown passes, receiver Gary Clark made the **Pro Bowl**, and the defense specialized in creating **turnovers**.

In the playoffs, Washington overpowered the Atlanta Falcons and then the Detroit Lions. The Redskins met the Buffalo Bills in Super Bowl XXVI. Washington confused Buffalo with a **no-huddle offense** and flooded the field with four and five receivers on many plays.

Rypien had a great game, but the Washington defense was the difference. The Redskins **intercepted** four passes and held star running back Thurman Thomas to just 13 yards. Washington led 24–0 in the third quarter and cruised to victory from there.

LEFT: Doug Williams fires a pass against the Denver Broncos.
ABOVE: Mark Rypien celebrates a touchdown against the Buffalo Bills.

To be a true star in the NFL, you need more than fast feet and a big body. You have to be a "go-to guy"—someone the coach wants on the field at the end of a big game. Redskins fans have had a lot to cheer about over the years, including these great stars …

THE PIONEERS

CLIFF BATTLES   Running Back

- BORN: 5/1/1910 • DIED: 4/28/1981
- PLAYED FOR TEAM: 1932 TO 1937

Cliff Battles led the NFL in rushing twice and was the first player to run for 200 yards in a game. Battles retired in 1938 after an argument over his salary. In six seasons, he was voted **All-Pro** three times.

SAMMY BAUGH   Quarterback/Punter

- BORN: 3/17/1914 • DIED: 12/17/2008 • PLAYED FOR TEAM: 1937 TO 1952

Sammy Baugh could do it all. In 1943, he led the NFL in passing, punting, and interceptions. During one game that season, he threw for four touchdowns and intercepted four passes. In 1947, Baugh became the first player to pass for more than 2,500 yards in a season.

BOBBY MITCHELL Receiver

• BORN: 6/6/1935 • PLAYED FOR TEAM: 1962 TO 1968

Bobby Mitchell was the Redskins' first African-American star. He was also one of the hardest players to tackle in NFL history. He led the league in catches once and receiving yards twice.

BOBBY MITCHELL
WASHINGTON REDSKINS   FLANKER

SONNY JURGENSEN Quarterback

• BORN: 8/23/1934 • PLAYED FOR TEAM: 1964 TO 1974

Sonny Jurgensen had a strong arm and an iron will. He waited until the last moment to throw his passes, knowing he was likely to be hit hard. Jurgensen led the NFL in passing yards three times with the Redskins.

CHARLEY TAYLOR Receiver

• BORN: 9/28/1941   • PLAYED FOR TEAM: 1964 TO 1977

Charley Taylor began his career as a running back. In 1966, the Redskins made him a receiver, and he led the NFL with 72 catches. When Taylor retired, he was first on the league's all-time list with 649 catches.

CHRIS HANBURGER Linebacker

• BORN: 8/13/1941 • PLAYED FOR TEAM: 1965 TO 1978

Chris Hanburger was captain of the Washington defense during the 1970s. He specialized in causing fumbles. Hanburger was voted into the **Hall of Fame** in 2011.

LEFT: Cliff Battles   **ABOVE:** Bobby Mitchell

JOE THEISMANN   Quarterback

- BORN: 9/9/1949   • PLAYED FOR TEAM: 1974 TO 1985

Some experts thought Joe Theismann was too small to play quarterback in the NFL. But they never measured the size of his heart. Theismann was named the NFL **Most Valuable Player (MVP)** in 1983.

JOHN RIGGINS   Running Back

- BORN: 8/4/1949   • PLAYED FOR TEAM: 1976 TO 1979 & 1981 TO 1985

John Riggins was big, strong, and very difficult to tackle. The Redskins gave him the ball when they needed tough yards. In 1983, Riggins set an NFL record with 24 touchdowns.

ART MONK   Receiver

- BORN: 12/5/1957   • PLAYED FOR TEAM: 1980 TO 1993

Art Monk was a master at using his body to create space for himself on the field. He often caught short passes and turned them into big gains. In 1992, Monk set an NFL record for most receptions in a career.

DARRELL GREEN   Defensive Back

- BORN: 2/15/1960   • PLAYED FOR TEAM: 1983 TO 2002

Darrell Green had blazing speed. He was also amazingly *durable*. Green intercepted at least one pass in 19 of his 20 seasons with the team.

CHAMP BAILEY

Defensive Back

- BORN: 6/22/1978   • PLAYED FOR TEAM: 1999 TO 2003

The Redskins took Champ Bailey with their first pick in the 1999 draft. He rewarded them with five spectacular seasons. Bailey made the Pro Bowl four times and had 18 interceptions. He even lined up as a receiver one season and caught three passes.

CHRIS SAMUELS   Offensive Lineman

- BORN: 7/28/1977
- PLAYED FOR TEAM: 2000 TO 2009

Chris Samuels was a huge blocker with great athletic ability. He could overpower opponents on running plays and pick up **blitzing** linebackers on pass plays. Samuels was picked for the Pro Bowl six times from 2001 to 2008.

SANTANA MOSS

Receiver

- BORN: 6/1/1979   • FIRST YEAR WITH TEAM: 2005

The Redskins traded for Santana Moss to give their offense a jolt of energy. In his first season, he caught 84 passes, scored nine touchdowns, and set a team record for receiving yards. In 2008, Moss returned a punt 80 yards for a touchdown. Three years later, he was made an offensive co-captain along with lineman Trent Williams.

LEFT: Darrell Green
ABOVE: Chris Samuels

Calling the Shots

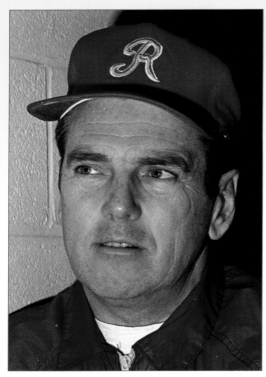

A good coach can make the difference between a winning season and a losing one. This has been especially true for the Redskins. Ray Flaherty took over the team in 1936 during its last season in Boston. In 1937, he led the team to the NFL title.

Flaherty had been a star receiver as a player. He was the perfect coach for Sammy Baugh. Flaherty taught Baugh the **screen pass**. Today, it is one of football's most exciting plays. The Redskins went to the championship game three more times under Flaherty and Baugh.

In 1969, the Redskins hired Vince Lombardi to whip their players into shape. Lombardi was one of the NFL's greatest coaches. Unfortunately, he coached for only one season. Lombardi was gravely ill and died in 1970. George Allen replaced

LEFT: George Allen
RIGHT: Joe Gibbs

him. He brought several veteran players to the team and guided the Redskins to the Super Bowl. Allen's teams were known as the "Over the Hill Gang."

Washington's greatest coach was Joe Gibbs. Before coming to the Redskins, he worked as an assistant under Don Coryell, a coach who loved to challenge defenses with a creative passing game. Gibbs used this **strategy** with Washington, but he also built a rugged running attack.

Gibbs coached the Redskins twice. From 1981 to 1992, Washington won the Super Bowl three times, and he was named Coach of the Year twice. In 2004, Gibbs agreed to return as coach. The Redskins had not had a winning season for four years. In 2006, they made it back to the playoffs.

One Great Day

Changing quarterbacks during the regular season is never an easy decision for a coach. Joe Gibbs faced this situation in 1987. Jay Schroeder was having a good year for the Redskins, but Gibbs thought the team would have more success with Doug Williams. As the playoffs began, he made the 32-year-old his starter. Williams responded with victories in two exciting playoff games. Next, the Redskins faced John Elway and the Denver Broncos in Super Bowl XXII.

The Broncos looked like the better team in the first quarter. Elway played brilliantly, and Denver took a 10–0 lead. That all changed in the second quarter. Williams hit Ricky Sanders for an 80-yard touchdown pass. A few minutes later, Gary Clark caught a pass from Williams for a 27-yard touchdown. The next time Washington had the ball, Timmy Smith ran for a 58-yard score. The Redskins weren't done. Williams and Sanders connected again, this time for a 50-yard touchdown. Just before halftime, Williams threw his fourth

Doug Williams tells Super Bowl photographers the Redskins are number one!

touchdown of the second quarter, to Clint Didier. In an amazing scoring burst, the Redskins put up 35 points—more than any team had scored in one quarter in the Super Bowl.

In the second half, Washington turned to its running game. Smith, a last-minute substitute for running back George Rogers, had the greatest game of his career. He finished with 204 yards to set a Super Bowl record. As the Redskins celebrated in the locker room, Gibbs looked like a genius. Washington won its fifth championship by a score of 42–10, thanks to two players who barely played during the regular season.

Legend Has It

Who was the most superstitious Redskin?

LEGEND HAS IT that Joe Theismann was. Theismann had to go through a series *rituals* before every game. The night before, he had to eat a banana split. On game day, he always had pancakes and scrambled eggs for breakfast and then traveled to the stadium with teammates Mark Moseley and Dave Butz. Theismann got to the locker room early enough to read *People* magazine all the way through, but he would not get his ankles taped until everyone else on the team had done so.

ABOVE: Joe Theismann

Did the Redskins once run out of footballs?

that they did. In a 1966 game at RFK Stadium, the Redskins and New York Giants set a record with 113 points. Washington won, 72–41. Kicker Charlie Gogolak booted so many **extra points** into the stands that the team ran out of extra balls. Gogolak's final kick was a **field goal** as time ran out. That ball was the last one left!

Did a Washington player once suffer a career-ending injury before a game?

that Turk Edwards did. Edwards was an offensive lineman and a leader for Washington. As captain of the Redskins, it was his job to go out on the field for the coin toss before each game. Prior to a game in 1940, Edwards called the toss, shook hands with the captains of the other team, and turned back toward the Washington bench. As he did, his cleats caught in the grass and his knee gave out. Edwards never played again.

The 1987 NFL season was one of the weirdest on record. A dispute between team owners and players led to a **strike** that lasted nearly a month. During that time the games continued—with replacement players!

Coach Joe Gibbs faced one of the biggest challenges of his career with the Redskins. His replacement players were a mismatched bunch made up of former high school and college stars. All were living out their dreams. To the amazement of the Washington fans, the Redskins won all three of their games with replacements.

On October 19, the Redskins faced the Dallas Cowboys. Gibbs knew his team was in for a tough battle.

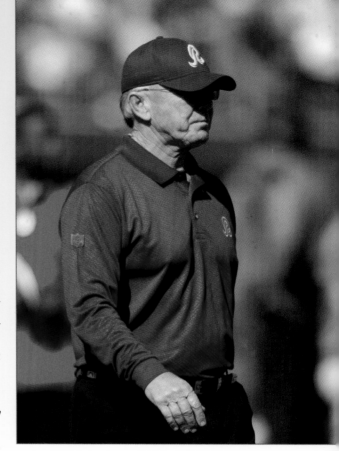

LEFT: Danny White could not get in a groove against the Redskins.
RIGHT: Joe Gibbs watches his team practice. Washington's victory over the Dallas Cowboys in 1987 was one of his finest moments.

Several Dallas stars were in uniform, including running back Tony Dorsett, quarterback Danny White, and a handful of defensive players. All week long, NFL fans wondered how badly the Redskins would get beaten. Some were saying the score might be 100–0!

The game was aired on *Monday Night Football*. All eyes were on quarterback Tony Robinson. He was playing instead of the injured starter, Ed Rubbert. Robinson had not played much football since college. In fact, he had recently been released from prison.

The Washington replacements banded together in the face of impossible odds. Meanwhile, the Cowboys were disorganized and ***frustrated***. Robinson led the Redskins to a 13–7 victory. Years later, this story inspired a movie called *The Replacements*, starring Keanu Reeves.

Tradition is everything to Redskins fans. They have been cheering for their marching band since 1937. They have been singing the team's fight song, "Hail to the Redskins," since 1938. In 1962, the Redskins formed an official cheerleading squad. It has been performing for fans ever since—longer than any other group in the NFL.

The loyalty of Washington fans has made the team one of the most valuable in sports. When Daniel Snyder bought the Redskins and their stadium in 1999, it cost him $800 million. That was one of the biggest price tags in league history. Washington's proud history of winning also contributes to the team's value. The Redskins have long been the favorite team of fans from Delaware to Florida. Many continued rooting for Washington even after other teams started playing in the mid-Atlantic region.

LEFT: Washington fans root for their beloved Redskins.
ABOVE: Fans wore this stadium pin during the 1960s

Timeline

n this timeline, each Super Bowl is listed under the year it was played. Remember that the Super Bowl is held early in the year and is actually part of the previous season. For example, Super Bowl XLVI was played on February 5, 2012, but it was the championship of the 2011 NFL season.

1937
The Redskins win their first NFL championship.

1972
Billy Kilmer ties for the NFL lead in touchdown passes.

1932
The team plays its first season, as the Boston Braves.

1942
The Redskins win their second NFL championship.

1957
Gene Brito is named All-Pro for the third time.

Sammy Baugh led the team to NFL titles in 1937 and 1942.

Gene Brito

Gene Brito

END-REDSKINS

Mark
Moseley

Mark Rypien led
the team to
victory in the
Super Bowl
in 1992.

1982
Kicker Mark Moseley
is named NFL MVP.

1992
The Redskins win their
fifth NFL championship.

2010
Mike Shanahan
is hired as coach.

1988
The Redskins win their
second Super Bowl.

1999
Stephen Davis scores
17 touchdowns.

2007
Chris Cooley is voted to the
Pro Bowl for the first time.

Chris
Cooley

Fun Facts

NAME GAME

Sammy Baugh was known as "Slingin' Sammy." He could also have been called "Bootin' Baugh" because he was probably the greatest punter in NFL history. He could kick the ball more than 60 yards, even while on the run. Baugh led the league in punting four times.

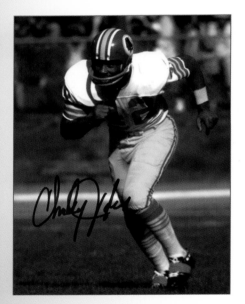

DOUBLE TROUBLE

In 1964, Charley Taylor gained 755 yards as a rusher and 814 yards as a receiver. It was the first time since the 1940s that a rookie had finished in the Top 10 in both running and receiving.

STEPPING ACROSS THE LINE

When the Redskins drafted Gene Brito in 1951, they thought he would make a fine receiver. They soon realized he was on the wrong side of the ball. Brito switched positions to defensive end and was named All-Pro three times.

ABOVE: Charley Taylor
RIGHT: John Riggins

EXPECT THE UNEXPECTED

John Riggins loved to do the opposite of what people expected—on the field and off it. Once when the team held a "casual dress" party, Riggins showed up in a white tuxedo with a top hat and walking stick.

QUIET HERO

Larry Brown was one of the best—and most courageous—players in team history. Brown was hearing impaired and needed a special device installed in his helmet so he could listen to plays in the huddle and signals on the field. He was named NFL MVP in 1972.

READ ALL ABOUT IT

During the 1980s, Dexter Manley became an inspiration to thousands of children and adults when he admitted that he could not read. Manley vowed to learn how and did so before his 30th birthday.

EDDIE LeBARON
QUARTERBACK   WASHINGTON REDSKINS

"He could always find a way to throw it off-balance. I've seen him throw the ball overarm, sidearm, and underarm and complete them."

▶ *Eddie LeBaron,* on Sammy Baugh

"I've always said that quarterback is an easy position to play until it becomes your job. Now, you have the responsibility of leading the team."

▶ *Sonny Jurgensen,* on the pressure of being a pro quarterback

"He was one of those guys who knew exactly how to play to the crowd. There are probably a million John Riggins stories—and all of them are true!"

▶ *Joe Gibbs,* on his favorite running back

"I've never been one to be caught up in stats. What's important is working hard, helping the team, and doing everything you can to win."

▶ **Art Monk,** *on achieving team goals instead of personal ones*

"I don't think you see that kind of football every day. How do I explain it? I guess with a 'wow' or an 'awesome.' There's no other way to do it."

▶ **Doug Williams,** *on the second quarter of Super Bowl XXII*

"I'm honest, I'm faithful, I've been responsible. My kids can find a hero right here, and it's not because I can run up and down the field."

▶ **Darrell Green,** *on being a role model off the football field*

LEFT: Eddie LeBaron   **ABOVE**: Art Monk

Great Debates

People who root for the Redskins love to compare their favorite moments, teams, and players. Some debates have been going on for years! How would you settle these classic football arguments?

The 1942 Redskins would beat any of Joe Gibbs's Super Bowl teams ...

... because they were one bad play away from an unbeaten season. Washington lost just one game that season on the way to the NFL championship. It came in the second week of the season. In a game against New York, the Giants returned an interception 66 yards for a touchdown. That was the difference in the loss. Sammy Baugh and the Redskins were that close to being perfect.

Oh, yeah? Any of those Super Bowl teams would whip the '42 Redskins ...

... because Joe Gibbs coached the Redskins to avoid mistakes and take advantage of errors by their opponents. Those teams also had great talent up and down the roster. By contrast, a lot of good players for Washington in the 1940s had already gone off to fight in World War II. With stars such as Joe Theismann, Doug Williams, John Riggins, and Art Monk (LEFT), the Redskins had too much firepower under Gibbs.

.. because it took two or three tacklers to bring him down. Riggins got the ball whenever the game was on the line—especially near the goal line. In Super Bowl XVII, Washington gave him the ball 38 times, and he gained 166 yards. Both were Super Bowl records. And, unlike other running backs, Riggins actually got better as he got older.

They don't come any tougher than Larry Brown ...

.. because he hit tacklers harder than they hit him. It was something to see! Brown (RIGHT) was picked to go to the Pro Bowl in each of his first four seasons. He was also named All-Pro twice. In 1972, he led the Redskins to the Super Bowl. Brown did all this despite wearing a hearing aid that helped him hear the quarterback's signals.

For the Record

The great Redskins teams and players have left their marks on the record books. These are the "best of the best" ...

Larry Brown

Joe Theismann

REDSKINS AWARD WINNERS

WINNER	AWARD	YEAR
Gene Brito	Pro Bowl co-MVP	1958
Charley Taylor	NFL Rookie of the Year	1964
George Allen	NFL Coach of the Year	1971
Larry Brown	NFL Most Valuable Player	1972
Mike Thomas	NFL Offensive Rookie of the Year	1975
Mark Moseley	NFL Most Valuable Player	1982
Joe Theismann	NFL Offensive Player of the Year	1983
Joe Theismann	NFL Most Valuable Player	1983
John Riggins	Super Bowl XVII MVP	1983
Joe Theismann	Pro Bowl MVP	1984
Doug Williams	Super Bowl XXII MVP	1988
Mark Rypien	Super Bowl XXVI MVP	1992

John Riggins

REDSKINS ACHIEVEMENTS

ACHIEVEMENT	YEAR
NFL Eastern Division Champions	1936
NFL Eastern Division Champions	1937
NFL Champions	1937
NFL Eastern Division Champions	1940
NFL Eastern Division Champions	1942
NFL Champions	1942
NFL Eastern Division Champions	1943
NFL Eastern Division Champions	1945
NFL Eastern Division Champions	1972
NFC Champions	1972
NFC Champions	1982
Super Bowl XVII Champions	1982*
NFL Eastern Division Champions	1983
NFC Champions	1983
NFL Eastern Division Champions	1984
NFL Eastern Division Champions	1987
NFC Champions	1987
Super Bowl XXII Champions	1987*
NFL Eastern Division Champions	1991
NFC Champions	1991
Super Bowl XXVI Champions	1991*
NFL Eastern Division Champions	1999

Super Bowls are played early the following year, but the game is counted as the championship of this season.

ABOVE: Shawn Springs was a leader of the 1999 NFC East champs.
LEFT: Fans bought this Redskins pennant in the 1940s.

Pinpoints

The history of a football team is made up of many smaller stories. These stories take place all over the map—not just in the city a team calls "home." Match the pushpins on these maps to the **Team Facts**, and you will begin to see the story of the Redskins unfold!

TEAM FACTS

1 Washington, D.C.—*The Redskins have played in this area since 1937.*

2 Boston, Massachusetts—*The team played here from 1932 to 1936.*

3 Mocksville, North Carolina—*Joe Gibbs was born here.*

4 Zachary, Louisiana—*Doug Williams was born here.*

5 White Plains, New York—*Art Monk was born here.*

6 Muncie, Indiana—*Ryan Kerrigan was born here.*

7 Houston, Texas—*Brian Orakpo was born here.*

8 Spokane, Washington—*Ray Flaherty was born here.*

9 St. Edward, Nebraska—*Pat Fischer was born here.*

10 Pasadena, California—*The Redskins won Super Bowl XVII here.*

11 Minneapolis, Minnesota—*The Redskins won Super Bowl XXVI here.*

12 Rabahidveg, Hungary—*Charlie Gogolak was born here.*

Brian Orakpo

Glossary

Football Words
Vocabulary Words

ALL-PRO—An honor given to the best players at their positions at the end of each season.

BACKFIELD—The players who line up behind the line of scrimmage. On offense, the quarterback and running backs are in the backfield.

BLITZING—Rushing the quarterback with extra players.

BURGUNDY—A deep red color named after a type of wine.

DECADE—A period of 10 years; also a specific period, such as the 1950s.

DRAFT—The annual meeting during which NFL teams choose from a group of the best college players.

DURABLE—Able to avoid or withstand injury.

EAST DIVISION—A group of teams that play in the eastern part of the country.

EXTRA POINTS—Kicks worth one point, attempted after a touchdown.

FIELD GOAL—A goal from the field, kicked over the crossbar and between the goal posts. A field goal is worth three points.

FRUSTRATED—Disappointed and puzzled.

GREAT DEPRESSION—The economic crisis that started in 1929 and lasted until the 1940s.

HALL OF FAME—The museum in Canton, Ohio, where football's greatest players are honored.

INTERCEPTED—Caught in the air by a defensive player.

LOGO—A symbol or design that represents a company or team.

MOST VALUABLE PLAYER (MVP)—The award given each year to the league's best player; also given to the best player in the Super Bowl and Pro Bowl.

NATIONAL FOOTBALL CONFERENCE (NFC)—One of two groups of teams that make up the NFL.

NATIONAL FOOTBALL LEAGUE (NFL)—The league that started in 1920 and is still operating today.

NFC EAST—A division for teams that play in the eastern part of the country.

NO-HUDDLE OFFENSE—A method of calling plays in which the offense does not get into a huddle.

PLAYOFFS—The games played after the regular season to determine which teams play in the Super Bowl.

PRO BOWL—The NFL's all-star game, played after the regular season.

PROFESSIONAL—Paid to play.

RITUALS—Procedures that are done the same way again and again.

ROOKIES—Players in their first season.

SCREEN PASS—A short pass thrown to a player with a protective "screen" of blockers in front of him.

SECOND WIND—A return of energy or strength.

STRATEGY—A plan or method for succeeding.

STRIKE—A work stoppage by employees.

SUPER BOWL—The championship of the NFL, played between the winners of the National Football Conference and American Football Conference.

SUPERSTITION—A trust in magic or luck.

SYMBOLIZES—Represents a thought or idea.

TRADITION—A belief or custom that is handed down from generation to generation.

TURNOVERS—Fumbles or interceptions that give possession of the ball to the opposing team.

VETERAN—Experienced.

WORLD WAR II—The war among the major powers of Europe, Asia, and North America that lasted from 1939 to 1945. The United States entered the war in 1941.

OVERTIME

TEAM SPIRIT introduces a great way to stay up to date with your team! Visit our **OVERTIME** link and get connected to the latest and greatest updates. **OVERTIME** serves as a young reader's ticket to an exclusive web page—with more stories, fun facts, team records, and photos of the Redskins. Content is updated during and after each season. The **OVERTIME** feature also enables readers to send comments and letters to the author! Log onto:

www.norwoodhousepress.com/library.aspx

and click on the tab: **TEAM SPIRIT** to access **OVERTIME**.

Read all the books in the series to learn more about professional sports. For a complete listing of the baseball, basketball, football, and hockey teams in the **TEAM SPIRIT** series, visit our website at:

www.norwoodhousepress.com/library.aspx

On the Road

WASHINGTON REDSKINS
1600 FedEx Way
Landover, Maryland 20785
703-726-7000
www.redskins.com

THE PRO FOOTBALL HALL OF FAME
2121 George Halas Drive NW
Canton, Ohio 44708
330-456-8207
www.profootballhof.com

On the Bookshelf

To learn more about the sport of football, look for these books at your library or bookstore:

- Frederick, Shane. *The Best of Everything Football Book.* North Mankato, Minnesota: Capstone Press, 2011.

- Jacobs, Greg. *The Everything Kids' Football Book: The All-Time Greats, Legendary Teams, Today's Superstars—And Tips on Playing Like a Pro.* Avon, Massachusetts: Adams Media Corporation, 2010.

- Editors of *Sports Illustrated for Kids. 1st and 10: Top 10 Lists of Everything in Football.* New York, New York: Sports Illustrated Books, 2011.

Index

About the Author

MARK STEWART has written more than 50 books on football and over 150 sports books for kids. He grew up in New York City during the 1960s rooting for the Giants and Jets, and was lucky enough to meet players from both teams. Mark comes from a family of writers. His grandfather was Sunday Editor of *The New York Times,* and his mother was Articles Editor of *Ladies' Home Journal* and *McCall's.* Mark has profiled hundreds of athletes over the past 25 years. He has also written several books about his native New York and New Jersey, his home today. Mark is a graduate of Duke University, with a degree in history. He lives and works in a home overlooking Sandy Hook, New Jersey. You can contact Mark through the Norwood House Press website.

ML

9-15